In Between Winter and Dawn

In Between Winter and Dawn

William O'Neal II

ISBN 978-1984127938

Edited by: Angela Watford & Matthew Huff

Front and back cover illustrations by: Jaida Condo

Printed in the United States of America

First Printing, 2018

Published by William O'Neal II

P.O. Box 1451

Fairburn, GA, USA 30213

For everyone stuck in winter,

patiently awaiting a new dawn

Contents

Part One: Winter

Broken Heartstrings...1

Sincerely.. 2

Green Apples.. 3

Penny Picture.. 5

Too Much Responsibility.. 8

A Borrowed Pen.. 9

False God..11

Merry-Go-Round... 12

Painkillers.. 13

Trampled Flowers.. 14

Hindsight Nightmares... 16

Parachutes... 18

Illogical Love.. 20

Band-Aids.. 21

Battle Plans.. 22

Awake... 25

This Poem is Not About Ceramic Plates..................................... 26

Champagne and Pools.. 28

Brothers With Bullets and Holes... 29

Drinking About You... 30

Fear Imagined.. 31

Sixty-Five Roses... 32

Expectations.. 34

Fine Wine and Paper Cups.. 35

No Promises.. 37

Do Not Disturb... 39

Over You... 40

Midnight Sandcastles.. 41

Whiskey.. 43

Masquerade... 44

In Between Winter and Dawn.. 46

Part Two: Dawn

Pixie Dust... 48

Cutting Diamonds... 49

Keys... 50

The Magician... 51

Greedy Polaroid... 53

She'll See You.. 54

Kissing Through The Glass.. 56

White Picket Fence... 58

Stay... 59

No Regrets... 60

I'm Red and You're Pink... 61

The Abandoned House on Broad Street................................ 62

The Wishing Well... 63

Redeem Me in Threes... 64

Worth.. 67

The Doctor.. 69

Sails.. 72

Twenty Below.. 73

Red Lipstick.. 74

A Prayer... 75

Creation... 76

Lampshade... 77

Graveyard Waltz.. 78

Morning Routine.. 79

Rooftop Garden... 80

Breakfast With God.. 82

My Imaginary Friend.. 85

Painting by Numbers.. 86

"So he tasted the deep pain that is reserved only for the strong, just as he had tasted for a little while the deep happiness."
— F. Scott Fitzgerald, All the Sad Young Men

Winter

Broken Heartstrings

A heart breaks in fourths.

Now, all the music makes sense:

Notes fine-tuned for pain.

Sincerely

I'm happy for you…

followed by a less than sign,

paired with a number three,

written with tears of ink.

Green Apples

The rooster crows at six o'clock
on Tuesday morning.
The plastic coffee pot — dry.
Unopened envelopes imitate mountains
next to a dull mail opener
and tomorrow is Wednesday.

An older gentleman wakes
to the sound of a taunting rooster
and can feel his own present pour
through the crevices of his time-stained hands —
dirt, heartbreak, and decades buried
beneath his fingertips.

He lives modestly, but alone.
He sleeps with his doors unlocked
and a gun in his sock drawer.
He buys birthday presents every
year but never expects to receive any.
Balancing his time in a life cut
short, he often sings ballads in the shower.

He is not a gardener, yet
he crouches on his knees,
to dig miles of holes

with a hand shovel, planting two

apple seeds in each.

He's not much of a gardener,

but he maximizes his time

the best way he knows how.

He often finds himself standing

over an empty kitchen sink

with a shot glass and a green apple,

because he believes

an apple a day, keeps the reaper away.

Every night, the gentleman says

a prayer, lies sideways on his full-sized mattress,

head upon his hands,

and wonders how much time will pass before

the rooster crows again in the morning.

Penny Picture

She is grace and she is beauty,
but these qualities weren't *pretty*
enough for the public's viewing.
So they paint, Photoshop, and cut
her image so it's picture perfect
for the movie screenings.

Now everyone's buying a ticket
to the free entertainment,
purchasing an image they can never
really obtain. But, they will try anyway.

Deciding whether there will be a second date,
by her dress size and not her passions
and the way they radiate her face.

So boys are blooming into men
looking for a wife to have maybe one
or two kids, and become disenchanted
with baby bottles, diapers and baby feet
in the face while in bed.

Now I'm guilty, just as guilty as the
guy next to me, eyes glued to the computer

screen, hoping his broadband dreams transpose
to reality and it's only when I crack my screen
that I see that I'm broken with lustful tendencies —
viewing her as an image beneath my fingertips.

I apologize by deleting the browser history.

Sex is no longer a bridge between souls
but a listing on a résumé to *out-do*
the other guy whose currently *winning,*
even though he's married with two children
and a dog named Penny.

And so on his scheduled once-a-month date,
he walks behind instead of holding her hand
side-by-side, hoping for a view equal to
the image on his iPhone 5.

And so while we lower our standards
to the bar with cheap conversations
and read between the line intentions,
we have no desire for a life-long commitment.

She looks in the mirror and wonders why
her life is so different from her husband's
expectations.

So she abandons her love for the dance floor,
writing, playing Legos with her kids at five,
building bookshelves and reading 'til she's tired
to provide a feeling she only felt before the
vowels in her vows:

"I do."

The absurdity of pornography is the hole it digs
while trying to fill it simultaneously.

Now, all that's left are hungry hands
on the prowl for women, their bodies
and feelings disguised as love,
until the high fades —

leaving a half-empty bed,
three vacant rooms,
a doghouse
and the agony of silence.

Too Much Responsibility

Today, I stumbled over a beating

heart on the sidewalk corner

of 5th and 6th Avenue. I didn't bother

to pick it up because the one

I was carrying was heavy enough.

A Borrowed Pen

If I paint you with poetry
will your figure resemble the form of my stanzas?
Will your presence give my breath pause
like a comma breaks a sentence?
Can we stare at each other for hours,
not say a word yet read each other
like my tattered edition of *Goodnight Moon?*
Ink and silence bleeding through every other page.

Will you snore like a misspelled word?
Dance as though a 1st grader were drawing
your steps in cursive —
and dream in cartoons?

I don't know.
I don't know.

I remember sitting across from you,
your eyes — blots of blue ink
writing stories and creating worlds like gods.

I can't be your author,
for this pen doesn't belong to me,
but I hope our stories fall parallel
with no chapter headings

or blank pages in between.

We will clash like a run-on novel,
and I will love you
like a first draft —
without the spell-check.

False God

Behind the masquerade of a preacher's son,

lies hurt and pain just like the rest of

the congregation, but they keep looking

for him to teach them how to make no mistakes.

They will soon wake to newspaper headlines

that their *Superman* is actually Lois Lane.

Merry-Go-Round

You tell me his name

and suddenly at 2 PM

in the afternoon, I feel drunker

than the night I fell in

love for the first time,

only now I want my world

to stop spinning.

Painkillers

The heart is not meant to heal fully.

If it were, we would become numb to pain

and there would be no need for

a doctor.

Trampled Flowers

I only cry under pink skies that

Rain down white petals of

Chamomile at night,

when the moon can only see half my face

and I can see half of hers.

When I moved from under the roof

of my parents' home,

I told my dad I didn't want his

hand-me-down shoes, old neckties

nor his time. I want to earn my own.

I asked my mother to close the fables by Aesop

and to no longer write me lunch notes with

her flowery bank pen

as I rearranged the sheets she carefully tucked me into.

I left trampled gerberas

and smeared kisses from my cheek

at their feet

tied to the end of a dead phone line.

Gradually do the seasons change

from full bronze decorating bouquets of violet Asters

to fading sunflowers and brisk air.

To dying marigolds and falling
snowflakes onto black peonies
morphing into white snowdrops.

To new life, budding daisies and
more chamomile sheltering my seawater brimmed eyes
with waxy fingers and a delicate touch,
masking broken bridges from those
who linger by with untied shoelaces and mismatched socks.

Childishly did I change the season
of home-cooked meals
and washed clothes with two drier sheets

using the lack of
three words that scraped
its hidden thorns back down my throat,

I love you.
I refused to speak to my parents, so

falling into brisk air and
over brown sunflowers,
I watered all the blossoms that I trampled
with silent tears and thanked them
for its dead roots I soaked with salt.

Hindsight Nightmares

It wasn't until I was forced to look back
over my chipped shoulder, that I realized
how close to the edge we were standing.

Ma, when you sat us down and explained
the hellish war we were about to engage in,
I was only partially armored.

Unprepared.

My heart was left vulnerable to the arrows of loss
and blows of reality that the enemy had mapped out for us.
Honestly, I didn't really grasp the depth of our condition
until it started to take a toll on you and even then
I was frozen in a false complacency.

To me, you were invincible.

Just the idea of anything being able to infiltrate
your thick, handcrafted skin was inconceivable.

Now, every time I close my eyes that pink
ribbon of hope turns into a noose and threatens
to suffocate me, but before the bucket is kicked
I wake in cold sweats.

I am content in my nightmares,

because even in your weakest moments,

you possess a strength and embody a state

of peace, that I can only dream of.

Parachutes

You stood on the ground, smiling,
head up, waiting for me to jump
from atop the highest mountain of
your heart. Rose-gold mountains,
your favorite color, capped with
blue snow and white flowers.

Your mountains, a view to die for, but

the altitude reached too far into heaven,
I had no choice but to dive forwards
to avoid suffocation. I fell thousands
of feet into thin air in front of pink
mountains with no intentions of
saving myself —

with coordinates directly aimed to crash
into a net of your hair.

Two years later, when falling felt the same
as waiting and your eyes were no longer
guiding me, I pulled the safety strap
of a parachute and steered myself safely
to the ground.

I fell in between me and you
for as long as there was room
for me to breathe, but free-falling
is not easy when it costs everything.

I'm sorry I chose
a parachute instead of us
but I would have kept falling
if you cared whether I saved myself
or fell for you.

Illogical Love

If we tried to reason with Love,

it would run circles 'round us

until we were just dizzy enough,

to fall into it.

Band-Aids

Masking knee-deep wounds,

ripping hairs from cocoa skin;

a double-edged sword.

Battle Plans

Men, today we go to war.
Today, we storm the white, sandy beaches
of Normandy, fly P-51s overhead past enemy lines,
take root deep in the crowded trenches
and follow in the triumph and tragic stories
of your fellow soldiers who have gone before you.

The Sergeant spoke with such a tone
that if faced with a platoon of light-headed
toddlers, his voice alone would frighten
their crooked, flashy and spotty grins
into their respective places.

I do warn you, he beckoned,
the task at hand is not for the faint of heart.
But for those who long to earn the title of
"Knight in Shining Armor" must first mount
their stallion, strap up their boots, and rescue
their princess from the dragon's layer,
winning over her heart with the intensity of his own.

I can't lie, the words shooting out of the
Sergeant's mouth like a firing squad
were intimidating.

However,
I knew she was worth the second guesses, nervous ticks,
skipped heartbeats, sweaty palms, reoccurring dreams,
overpriced coffee, the late nights, long conversations,
vows of honesty
and everything that was bound to come.

So men, when you stand at the base of the towering castle
having crossed the mote of raging lava,
slain the mouth-breathing dragon,
and evaded the infamous friend zone —
a war that no man has come out alive
and climbed the spiraling staircase to the uppermost room
know that the battle has just begun.

For when you open the unlatched wooden door
and find her standing at the window,
her back to you with the sunlight perfectly outlining her figure,
know that you have finally met your match.

Her presence alone
has the capability to cause your heart to mimic
three days without sleep and a surge of adrenaline.

When she turns around,
spinning the world with her,

immediately look away,

for her smile has the power to fully paralyze you.

Men, I am sorry.

And with a look of sincerity,

he confessed,

The way to victory is found only through surrender.

For when you show your beloved, you will sacrifice glory

for her sake, she will entrust you with everything.

But with tears in his eyes and regret in his heart,

the Sergeant urged every soldier to examine his battle plans.

Once you hold the heart to the one you love,

dare not to drop it and

protect it as if it is your own. —

for if the love is true,

when one heart breaks

the other follows suit.

Awake

It was all a dream.

I know, because when I fell

I opened my eyes.

This Poem is Not About Ceramic Plates

I stand in the kitchen, with long
shoelaces tied together, butter
smeared on the palm of my hands,
in between my fingers, standing
on one foot while holding one
ceramic plate with two fists.

Beads of sweat chase each other
down the center of my forehead
and my legs shake as a perfect
plate crashes, shatters and breaks
apart on the hardwood kitchen floor.

Months, I spent on my knees
begging and piecing back together
the broken pieces with scotch tape,
Elmer's glue and half sticks of chewed
gum.

Giving up: The ceramic plate never
smiled again after I pleaded for her
to fix herself. I never ate with it again,
always too hesitant to hold it close anymore.
My kitchen is now nothing
but an empty sink and shelves

of disposable paper plates that

begin to overflow in recycle bins.

Champagne and Pools

I drown my demons

in a pool of champagne foam;

we all raise a glass.

Brothers With Bullets and Holes

You hid the gun and bouquet of bullets in my hand,
we went to war against Cerberus together, yet
we were nothing but an hourglass: waterfalls of sand.

Brother, we dug trenches and commanded the land,
your shoulder, carved for my heavy head but
you hid the gun and bouquet of bullets in my hand.

Your laugh was an orchestrated band,
the enemy surrendered at every note, still
we were nothing but an hourglass: waterfalls of sand.

Standing at the gates of hell, we still found time to dance.
You were the lead and spun me around,
hiding the gun and bouquet of bullets in my hand.

I never questioned your left hand
when your right was guiding me,
we were nothing but an hourglass: waterfalls of sand.

From the beginning, your smile revealed nothing of our future.
I was damned, bleeding from the holes in my chest when we
first spoke:
You hid the gun and bouquet of bullets in my hand,
we were nothing but an hourglass: waterfalls of sand.

Drinking About You

I think about you more
than you know. I drink
about you too, stumbling
over every word we ever
spoke to each other.

Fear Imagined

Facing a white wall plastered with uncertainty,

the sleeping butterflies in his stomach

awaken into fire-breathing dragons.

The beating red rock in his chest begins

and then refuses to cease pounding against

a prison cage of bones. His throat filled

to the brim with tar, sticks to every chord

and word he wishes to speak.

Yet, he is complacent in his silence,

paralyzed by the world of his imagination.

He screams at himself,

closing his eyes to escape the madness

and quiet the noise —

he discovers the light.

Sixty-Five Roses

Three months in, he knocked at my door.
Well, more like barged in without warning.
Heaven knows without invitation.

Entering with a bouquet of roses,
sixty-five to be exact,
attempting to sweeten and soften the toll
he was soon to take on my life,
my breath was stolen and
laughs were broken.

Making himself at home,
he proceeds to make my heart his dwelling,
turning my aorta into a sitting lounge
and substituting my capacity to be loved
with the thorns from his roses.

Leeching off the air from my lungs,
feeding off the nutrients in my intestines
and sipping my blood from a warm mug,
he draws my lifeline,
freehanded.

My body has become his playground
and as we chased each other up and

down kiddie slides, across monkey

bars and through worm holes,

we grew up together.

I know his deepest of intentions

and he knows me like I know my reflection.

Sometimes I am made to believe we are the same.

However, over the years,

we have moved a lot,

from companions to close enemies.

I have tried to count the beauty in my disease.

But I now realize that the red roses

he seduced me with are just origami

foldings stained with crimson blood.

Expectations

I took a sip of water,
hoping it was lemonade.

You can only imagine,
the sour disappointment.

Fine Wine and Paper Cups

Hiding between the paper-thin sheets of night
when the birds stop singing
and the stars act as streetlights,
we bury our heads in the light of the moon.

From mirrored, glass bottles we poured
aged wine into paper cups
while our hourglass drained just as fast.

She rests her hand on the furred rug,
leaning on her own strength for support
and the ringed shadow of light on her
left hand blinds me.

She probably left her ring in the glove
compartment of her husband's Corvette
just to drive away from
her home, from her headaches.

I guess she needed a smoke break,
and for a moment the Moscato and I
replaced the empty box of Marlboros
sitting on the dashboard of her
all too familiar Chevrolet.

With her, conversations never looped,

wine never grew stale,

lipstick stained and teeth chipped

ninety-nine cent paper cups never ran short.

And laughs were never pretend,

unlike us.

She stood first,

handed me a folded letter

with the words *thank you* written

on the outside, placed a kiss of citrus

roses on my cheek

and left —

me, cleaning up mountains of paper cups

with hopes that she makes it back home, safely.

No Promises

You are blurry behind the tears
brimming above my eyelids but
I can see it. You, waltzing down
the aisle held in your father's arms
like you are twelve again.

My arms shaking in anticipation
of you falling into them and
trusting me to hold you steady
when our lips share one last
kiss apart.

I remember phone conversations
like yesterday when we were only
connected by the letters coursing
through our virtually intertwined
fingers.

Now the only thing keeping us apart
is the long embrace of your father
and the look of trust his tearful eyes
give mine.

We vow to love until death stops
our hearts and mine skipped a few

beats to remind me to cherish every
moment.

We are not promised a future and
the first tear falls from my eye to your
white dress, everything vanishes
and I am left standing in the mirror
with wishes that I was not
only dreaming but glimpsing
what is to come.

Do Not Disturb

Her words were a cornerstone of my home.

Through an iPhone, the light of her name sung.

When sleep, around my mind she danced and roamed —

leaving footprints of her name on my tongue.

Like sparks and oil drums, our music untamed,

her eyes were oceans and I longed to sink.

I failed to show my love and she felt shamed,

I wished to kiss and make her cheeks turn pink.

What could have been, haunts even the strongest man

and my past weeps for always wanting more.

My heart is numb yet beats on waves of sand,

I lie on a bare island with no shore.

> Left with a cracked phone screen and blank measures,
>
> a silent house drifts coldly untethered.

Over You

I will never be.

You smiled: slowly stole my heart,

please don't return it.

Midnight Sandcastles

The sun rises in the east and sets in the west, but
I choose to believe that time revolves around us.

As we sit on old, worn rocks that have been
forced to form billions of microscopic particles,
we are able to transpose our imagination into reality.
And the possibilities are endless.

I pass you my shovel
and we spend hours raising our own world.
We construct cathedrals, storefronts,
medieval empires, skyscrapers and skylines,
creating canvases for never-ending horizons.

I look over as the sun begins to set and as the sky
begins to grow dark, so does the smile on my face.
For I know that Father Time has co-signed our
expiration date right next to the signature
of our future.

So, I glance as pure light slowly meanders
down the side of your face, highlighting the
the string of hair glued to your lips,
and I capture every detail I can
with my faulty camera.

As the moon rises and the tide rolls in,
our memories along with our world
are washed away with the waves.

Nothing is left except for me
and the devastation of entire cities.

But, don't you worry,
I will begin to reconstruct
every street corner from scratch,
making up for every lost second

and hopefully you will return again,
come midnight tomorrow.

Whiskey

You fell on top of me
arms sprawled across my chest,
legs layered atop my torso
and deep breathes pressed
into my ear.

I didn't move and you couldn't either;
resting in a moment that would flee
as soon as my voice gave you a headache
the next morning.

Masquerade

The wealthy, the sane,

the damned, the poor,

the cheater, the judge,

the housemaid, the diligent,

the single wife, the victim,

the confident, the shameful,

the killer, the chef,

the consumer, the virgin,

the tired, the ambitious,

the broken-hearted, the Christian

the alcoholic, the actor,

the teacher, the adopted

the lover, the lonely,

the abused, the agnostic

the scared, the poet,

the politician, the powerless

and the fallen angel all dance

under broken moonlight shining

through stain glass windows;

all veiled behind bone-white
skin masques.

In Between Winter and Dawn

The moment in between winter

and dawn is when we learn

to wave snow angels into the

ground until the sun wakes from

behind the frost-bitten forest

to melt our pain.

Dawn

Pixie Dust

It's a guy's dream to make a girl
laugh, to see her lips widen
creating dimples, to hear kids
play pretend on her tongue,
throwing pixie dust from her
mouth as the wind blows it into
her clenched eyes and she
can barely walk.

She can't breathe and tears roll
from the corner of her eyes:
falling into the tall grass
as a new flower blooms
with every quarter note
that tumbles from her windpipe.

She then falls into his arms
and with her breath in his ear
the pixie dust whispers for another
joke so he tells the same one
because he doesn't know another
and she laughs again all the same.

Cutting Diamonds

Diamonds never realize they have been

cut, until they look into the mirror,

bouncing light into rainbows.

Keys

My hands dance across black keys
as if it is a grand piano,
creating melodies through stringed words
comprised of meticulous letters.

Taking hold of hearts
and a-trains of thought,
I beckon questions and encourage
the singing of new songs –

the songs of fingers interlocking,
the songs of children laughing,
the songs of cloudless rain,
the song of hate unloading,

spreading music through generations
and killing one-track minds,

turning loops into shuffles.

The Magician

"To the true magician disguised as my 12th grade literature teacher."

You've never seen a magician quite like this one.
Unlike other sleights of hand,
he doesn't grip a wand, instead
an arsenal of pens that wash
wonders onto blank pages.

He's no need putting on a show
or gimmicking to draw a
crowd, for people gather from miles
whenever there is a drawn curtain.

Common magicians always wear a top hat,
pulling white rabbits and rainbow ribbons out of thin air.

But a true magician hides in plain sight
using mere charm to captivate a crowd.

Look closely, he beckons.
Drawing his audience deeper in, but
widening their scope of imagination
for miles. Paving roads of passion, love,
and a hunger for truth.

You've never seen a magician quite like this one.
A magician who doesn't use magic at all,
but reveals the beauty of the real.

As the act comes to an end and the curtain closes,
the magician takes his final bow.

The audience is always left wanting more.

But when asked how his trick works,
he doesn't answer with:
A magician never reveals his secrets,

instead, hands every student a sorcery
pen and wells of ink knowing we will
never see the world the same again.

Greedy Polaroid

Give me one picture

that I can hold between

the fortune lines coursing

atop my shaky palm, so that

I can read our future while

opening my present.

She'll See You

Some day she will see you. She will see through the smoke screens and your poor pickup line. Your past will be revealed in her forgiving eyes, your present will be filled with *her* presence and your future will be yours together.

She will see that you are a mama's boy, but that you take after the gentleman nature of your father. She will see how you stand strong and hold back tears in the face of tragedy but open the floodgates when you believe no one is looking. She will learn to distinguish which tears are of joy and sadness. She will see the way you wander the streets at night just to look at the moon and brightness of the stars and hope that the cold air mixed with the light will frighten away your inner demons. She will see you.

She will witness the way you always lay your clothes out before your morning showers, get comfortable before eating a meal and how you sit in the driveway for ten minutes just to select the right music before driving off. She will see your relationship with your sister and how you annoy each other to the point of love. She will see and know the face when you are not aware of anything or anyone around you except the thoughts racing through the back of your mind. You won't be able to hide your favorite snacks behind the expired food in the pantry anymore and she will know your future goals like the passcode on her phone — and yours.

When you go to the movie theater she will see the ticket counter screen and know exactly what seats to reserve and which opening nights to look forward too. She will see the snowflakes falling from the heavens and know it is your favorite season because of the hoodie you've been waiting to wear all year. She will see your heart and the past relationships that have taken a toll on it.

She will see your two left feet on the dance floor, your weakest points and the insecurities never to mention in an argument, ever.

She will see whether you hug high or low, smile with your teeth or lips, and eat breakfast or brunch. She will know what nights will be long ones and see the clogs of your mind that will not let you rest. She will see the DVR and know which shows not to delete and which episodes of *How I Met Your Mother* you haven't seen. She will see a world map and be able to point out the parts of the world you constantly visit in your dreams. She will *see* you for who you truly are, not the person you wish you were. When she sees you, she will know how to love you. And you will never want to hide anything from her.

Kissing Through The Glass

The mahogany floor creaks
as two sets of bare feet play
follow the leader, toes quivering

as the frigid floor bears each hesitant
step only guided by a faint, half-burnt
candle stick. A tangled head
rests against a warm ear,

leaning with every move forward,
backward, side to side to side to,
repeating forward while Sinatra
pirouettes in the corner, leaping beautifully
over the needle of a dusty record player.

She places her polish-chipped fingers
inside his hand. He holds her gently,
caressing her waist without stunting
her breath. He misses a step,

Everybody loves somebody, sometime.
Everybody falls in love, somehow.

He whispered an apology and felt
both corners of her lips

widen as her teeth met his shoulder.
Then her head lifted and his eyes

met hers. Bare feet stopped cold in
their tracks and out of fear
they placed a sugar glass door
between them and stared into

each other with eight-ball pupils.
Steps danced closer together
as pink lips pressed smeared kisses on
washed thin glass. Hard-pressed longing

shattered maps of glass onto mahogany and
they shared sweet blood tainted
against red-stained teeth from glass
opened lips. Every other step, pained
by rigid corners under bare feet,
now stained crimson.

White Picket Fence

Every coat of paint that
I layer on chipped wood
reminds me of my father
and the pints of patience
he always placed at my
size 6 converse.

He said, "Paint the white fence
enough times and the grass
on your side will seem just as
green as the neighbors'."

It never made sense but I kept
painting strokes of white until
I no longer compared colors
or blades of grass

and I guess that's what he meant.

Stay

Pull your finger off the trigger,

drop the gun to the floor

and dirty your nails, digging

the bloodied bullet out

of your hardened chest.

Patch the hole with the silk threads

of your bed sheets and when

your mom asks where the scar

came from —

tell her you have more to give.

No Regrets

I looked at my scars

then looked up at the weapon

and I still loved her.

I'm Red and You're Pink

It wasn't until I was dancing

in my underwear, alone,

in my bedroom, at night

that I missed your skin on mine;

our hearts spinning and mixing

together like paint on white

bed sheets.

The Abandoned House on Broad Street

Alone she stands, away from prying eyes
and apart from the place of the commons.
With patched-up window panes and broken
glass bottles carelessly sprawled across her lawn,
she basks in the glorious rays of the tree-light's
fragmented sun.

Anyone who dares to visit the house of magnificent
horrors shall be overwhelmed by the truths hidden,
beneath the whispering floors.

There is much more than just rusted paint
and forgotten construction plans.

As the house cries out and sheds its worn skin,
signs of *warning* and *caution* of entry
plaster the beauty's stone-hard face;
a persona built to protect her heart of bonfire,
because one stone is all it takes to put it out.

Her window shutters are stamped with digits 187
but she is more than just a number.

The Wishing Well...

cried beautifully in the center
of attention and the lack there of:
Children with vanilla ice cream
painting their skin with melted
sugar and the frustrations of their
mother. Fathers, with patience as thin
as a tightrope but still just as flexible.

A rest at the wishing well with
bottom-of-the-purse pennies
and expensive quarters are tossed
carelessly into the shadowed water
of the well.

He knows he will always be half full
of water-thin wishes in exchange
for pennies and crumbled gum wrappers
but underwater, broken change still
glistens in the eye of a child's
wandering eyes.

That's enough to keep pouring
out waterfalls until he runs dry
only left with cheap wishes
and priceless smiles.

Redeem Me in Threes

Make me like Peter.

My hands are tied with fishnets of
glass-bottled Smirnoff on Fridays
featuring merry-go-round thoughts
that flow like water in a stream of stones,
and I question where I stand; as if I can stand
anywhere three shots ago much less now:
head tilted back, with a burning throat and eyes
clenched to God.

I was asked if I was a Christian and I responded
with a slurred *Yes* with an apostrophe *I think so*
attached to the end, not sure if God can see me
when I close my eyes.

Few days later, I walk a straight line back
to the steeple with a bible downloaded
on the same phone I relapsed on, the night
before. And when communion comes,
I drink the blood and eat the body and
it tastes fresh, stained by the Listerine I used
to censor my mistakes from three days ago.

Make me like Peter.

Let me deny you three times so that
I may be redeemed three more,
stretch me out and turn my body
upside down that I may imitate you
but not too perfectly because I will fail
every time.

Call me by the name you gave me,
let the tone of your voice unravel
the fishnets and shatter beneath my feet
spilling every word and period that did
not originate from the ball point of your
pen.

Let me know you by your voice and see
you through your miracles but love you
for the second chances in your eyes.

Make me like Peter.

Let me run towards you like a
drunkard, stumbling and falling
every three steps of the way like
my shoes are untied and on the wrong
feet. And when I'm too weak to stand,

may I crawl, head craned towards you,

never blinking with my eyes always in awe.

Worth

She deserves to have her heart
tattooed on her arm without
having to wear long sleeves
because of those who try
to claim the design as their own.

He deserves to cry rivers, on his
knees without being crowned
king of the damned; a boy with
a heart too soft to be a man.

She deserves to speak the ideas
that has settled in the back of her
mind with a megaphone loud enough
so the world listens, like a vinyl
on repeat that no one gets tired of.

He deserves the father that stays
around the campfire no matter how
cold the temperature drops, teaching
him how to wrap his sweater around
his little sister's shoulders and how to
bear the weather.
She deserves the guy who rolls
up her sleeve to make sure her

heart hasn't faded then intertwines

his arm with hers so they can swing to

the beat of the same drum

and never question whether they

are qualified to smile.

The Doctor

He sits, pen in hand and spectacles upright.

As he stares in silence,

the only visible sound is the stethoscope

swaying about his neck.

His hands are wrinkled,

as though time has tossed and turned,

unable to find rest upon a bed of stressed veins.

Still, they never cease to perform miracles.

I sit slouched on the exam table

with untied shoelaces and light-up sneakers

feeling as though my lungs are held

together with tar:

breath, short and air, limited.

When he walks into the room,

his cane sings a lullaby that quiets the world

with every other knock upon the tile floor.

Perceptive, evergreen eyes hide behind crooked bifocals.

As a light waves across my eye, I can catch a glimpse of the

world inside of his.

I picture a lone cabin in the midst of a grand wood.
Trees overarch high above the desolate chimney
but open just enough to invite beams of sunlight.

I'm lost in the brilliance of his mind,
but frightened when I spot
storm clouds protruding in the distance.

I panic and try to breathe deeply, again.
but I feel guilty,
the doctor treating me and
no one caring for him.

I read the aged lines of compassion on his face
and listen to the language of God on his tongue,
every time he whispers a prayer before entering the room.

And when I hear:
Take a deep breath, I do.
I know the sound of life
is his favorite song.

And though the doctor carries
the weight of the world,
all the lives which he has impacted
will never cease to stand beside him.

Every bed-ridden teenager, recovering cancer patient

and teary eyed child will never

fail in sheltering their savior's thoughts

from the thunderstorms that await *him*.

Sails

In your eyes I was always
the good sailor, floating
across your wide ocean-
green eyes.

Even after all of the storms
I sailed through and ships
that I sunk, you always
steadied my sails

by holding your breath around
me in hopes I would one day change.

The forgiveness that is the white foam
on the cuff of your sea guided me to shore
and when I buried my feet onto dry ground,

you were still waiting for me with open arms
and a relieved sigh warming the side of my neck.

Twenty Below

A pair of winter snow boots tiptoes
atop iced tennis shoes. Bare hands
intertwine black leather and
chapped lips quiver
icy breath.

Lips meet with layers
of chap stick, runny noses,
tears falling as snow thawing
into black asphalt.

They had become numb
to each other, gasping
for a kiss, a half burnt
cigarette, a bliss second of
touch;

trying to feel a remnant of
twenty years past when
hugs were warm and kisses
felt like the last missing piece
to a jigsaw puzzle.

Red Lipstick…

leaves permanent prints.

I hate red lipstick's boldness

except on her lips.

A Prayer

God, please place a smile

on her face instead of tears

even if I'm not the one that is

blinded by its radiance.

Creation

At the parting of His mouth,

oceans spilled, stars burned,

the winds conducted the song

of the birds, all was good

and God knew the fall of

perfection would be his last creation,

and yet He chose to keep speaking

until humanity was the last thought

that exhaled from His lips.

Lampshade

When the shadows seem
relentless and the lampshade
creates a dome of darkness
greater than the light, I take
a trip to the moon.

My back to the crater walls and
arms wrapped around hardened
knees I look up at the stars, brighter
and more magnificent than any
scar that shines on black skin.

And not even my grandmother's huge
lampshade I wore as an astronaut's
helmet when I was a kid could diminish
the starlight glazed over my eyes.

Graveyard Waltz

He blew the dirt from my eyes,
held my hands and craned my
stiff arms on His shoulder, laying
my limp forehead on His heart.

My heavy eyes kept wandering
to my grave of rest so He ripped
the gray stone from the cold soil
and placed it beneath our feet as a
proper dance floor.

*But is dancing really dancing if you're
dancing with a corpse?*

So, He called the moon closer
into a chandelier spotlight, gravity
lifted my head and my feet glistened
on engraved granite stone.

The tree branches played the strings
on graveyard gates and my eyes
followed His every step.

He waltzed with my dead body
and turned my mourning into dancing.

Morning Routine

Wake up and let your bare feet
touch, from heel to toe, the cold
ghastly floor in your chaotic bedroom.

Walk to the sink and wash the nightmares
from your eyes and let the hot shower water
thaw the winter from your frosted hair.

Line the toothbrush with the green mint strip
and brush the bitter words of yesterday off your tongue.
Brew the Wal-Mart brand coffee beans in your mom's
old coffee pot and pour it into the same mug you
use every day, from the last family trip to the mountains.

Wait for it to cool and tie your shoelaces, right foot first.
Bring the steaming mug to your pink lips and take a sip,
then swallow hard.

When the mint toothpaste mixes with the strong blend
and you clench your eyes, shrivel your tongue and
your throat tightens, breathe out and take another sip
until the mug is empty —
ready to face the day with minted coffee breaths.

Rooftop Garden

We rode the elevator to the 60th
floor: the only one with the rooftop access
and rooftop garden.

The sun was setting just as the elevator
doors were opening and your jaw dropped
as the sky painted your eyes with its own
colors of rusted orange, coloring-book purple
and parking-ticket yellow.

We walked through the garden and
sat on the ledge, feet dangling and
dancing over air with lack of safety nets.

I accidentally sat on a bed of lilies and you
shed a tear trying to stand them upright, again.

And when the stars finally appeared above us,
you couldn't help but stare, and I had the desire
to become an astronaut.

Without looking at me you asked,
What do you think Adam's first pickup line to Eve was?
I thought he probably lead her to all of the planets
and then pointed to the sixth one and said,

I will love you like God loved Saturn.

You looked at me with a huge grin on your face
and stardust stuck in between your teeth,

kissed me with honey-red lips,
snatched my hand into yours
and we ran across the rooftop
and through the garden, naked.

Breakfast With God

On Sunday morning,
God filled my bowl with golden
horizons instead of Rice Krispies.

My milk turned into dragon clouds
and then into bunny rabbits.

When I asked for a cup of coffee with two sugars,
He handed me a full pot with a bowl
of honey and an empty mug, but
He made me beg for a spoon.

Pancakes were inflated with
autumn air and the syrup was laced with
traces of leaves from the first maple tree.

We communed in a cabin, centered
in a part of the woods where no matter
the season, the trees were always full.

Inside, a round table draped with a white tablecloth
just short enough to kiss the floor without touching,
but long enough to hide my lost feet from showing.
On the other side of the table were pictures
of my mother,

my sister's worn *American Girl* doll
and the pocket watch my father
handcrafted for me.

Memories were all I had left
of my family —
they did not get an invite to breakfast.

Still, it felt like home, and I could wander
the woods and every perfect napping corner
of the cabin with closed eyes.

We didn't talk much, me always
with a mouth overflowing with jammed toast
and orange juice.

Used napkins scattered on the wooden floor
like a three year old,
nervous straws sat next to empty plates
and trains of crumbs next to a chipped coffee mug.

In the blink of my eye
orange juice, milk and honey
turned to thick cherry blood.
Strips of bacon appeared

to be scared human forearms,
pancakes turned to crowns
of thorns and sugar
was now salt.

I pushed back in a panic
from the table with no shoes and
a full yet weak stomach
and He smiled.

A smile that added hours to time by the second.
Eyes full of blue
and green oceans that could turn
black in an instant.
Yet, I knew all He wanted was to eat
breakfast with me, for every meal
of every day.

I didn't visit again until a week later —
I didn't deserve the breakfast, nor His treatment.
Yet, He still awaited my return.

That Sunday I decided to give
Him a second chance,
and we ate wedding cakes for breakfast.

My Imaginary Friend...

makes promises to me in ink
instead of pencil and never
leaves behind heavy blotches
of hesitation.

Others rarely see him but his voice
rests between the stitches of my
nighttime pillow. He walks beside
me, never a step behind and places
Legos in my hand to build a world
of our own.

He opened my eyes to the stars
when streetlights were what I
looked up to and stayed close
when others grew apart.

Although imaginary, he had skin
thicker than my mother and didn't
leave when I became too much
to bear.

Painting By Numbers

[co-written by: Gabrielle Cerasoli]

We started with our hands elbow deep in watercolor;

fresh eyed and ready to finger paint

first words, stick figures

and imaginary friends

who taught us how to redraw the single file lines

we were conditioned to stand in.

A pair of swings sway in harmony,

tying bonds between two elementary kids

who dared to fly.

But then recess and mud pie dates turned to

Romeo and Juliet romances,

imagination was standardized.

and we faced middle school

like a three year old

faces a 10,000-piece jigsaw puzzle.

Lost.

We tried to fit like the train tracks on our teeth,

where being cool was the phrase used to describe normal

and mirrors became close companions.

As we became closer, our friendship grew scarce,

bathroom mirrors contorted, betrayed us and

blew goodbye kisses to our pride.

Our reflections shattered and we walked across broken glass
so we bought the newest shoes to cover up the blood.

Lunch tables were quarantined
due to a cootie epidemic,
until a spark of an eye caused a revolution.

Together, two birds fell in love.
Hand in hand they joined the "dark side,"
(What middle schoolers refer to as love)
and stars began to fall,
illuminating everything in their path
and revealing where the light touches the earth.

Come high school,
with parental guided dates
and the world upside down,
we became kings and queens.
Cutting off long-standing relations and accepting others,
we each created royal courts,
each one claiming to be the fairest.

Lockers grew bare,

now filled only with old papers, candy wrappers and broken
pencils.
Abandoning combination locks and opening the door to our
pain,
we begin to accept the mess that we've made,
hoping that others will do the same.

Gossip turns to an open ear and a closed mouth,
because we begin to see ourselves in each other.
And so, empathy breeds compassion
but when that no longer suffices,
teachers intervene.

Our heroes of hope offer help with
an open door, an empty chair and thousands of miles
walked in shoes similar to our own,
acting as a crutch in our most vulnerable moments.

See, education is so much more than just variables,
historical dates, grammar and periodic tables.

Although we learn practicality
we discover principles.

Mathematics
is the language in which

God created the multiverse.

History,
the building block on which our future is built.

Chemistry and science,
proof of the majesty of God.

Literature and grammar,
a way in which we imitate the author of the universe,
while wallowing in the grandeur of truth.

So, we shouldn't be bored of education,
rather, use our middle school heartbreaks,
self-betrayals and friendship fallouts to color the
future ahead.

As we begin to dress in our caps and gowns,
say goodbye to people that we may not see for a while,
shake hands with those who have carried us this far,
look back at the memories and years that shaped us
and walk across the stage one last time –

we look down and notice that
the kindergarten watercolor
has dried on our adolescent hands.

So, our heroes covert our pain into color,

and as they continue to tell us how to

spread goodness, speak truth, and create beauty,

we are equipped with cans of spray paint

ready to brighten any gray cement walls

that tower above us —

though they may.

A message to you, the reader:

Thank you to all of you who used your hard earned money to buy this book. Personally, I write to convert all of my stress, anxiety and brokenness into beauty and use my talent to coherently express my thoughts. All of the poems in this book were written between the last two years and has helped me through a lot. It is my prayer and my wish that it also helps you and whomever you pass it along to, because that does so much more than these words merely sitting on my laptop computer. All of the profits of this book, no matter how many people buy it, will go directly to the foundation that helps patients with Cystic Fibrosis as well as a foundation that deals with suicide prevention. I believe my stories should be a light to those sitting in the dark and both foundations are very close to my heart.

Again, thank you all and I would like to encourage you to be intentional and to find the light when your eyes are blinded by the darkness in front of you. This life is worth living and you are worth the world and more, hopefully I am doing my part to help you see that. Live on, keep fighting, love deeply and keep forgiving.

With all the love and sincerity I have,
—Will

Made in the USA
Columbia, SC
02 July 2018